# Woodpecker in the Backyard

Cathy Mania and Robert C. Mania Jr.

A Wildlife Conservation Society Book

**Franklin Watts**
A Division of Grolier Publishing
New York • London • Hong Kong • Sydney
Danbury, Connecticut

The Wildlife Conservation Society (WCS) is dedicated to protecting and promoting the world's wildlife and wilderness areas. Founded in 1895 as the New York Zoological Society, the organization operates the Bronx Zoo, New York Aquarium, Central Park Wildlife Center, Queens Wildlife Center, and Prospect Park Wildlife Center. WCS also operates St. Catherines Wildlife Center, which is located off the coast of Georgia. The scientists at this center raise and study a variety of threatened and endangered animals.

WCS currently sponsors more than 350 field projects in 52 countries. The goal of these projects is to save wild landscapes and the animals that depend on them. In addition, WCS's pioneering environmental education programs reach more than 3 million students in the New York metropolitan area and are used in all 50 states and 14 foreign nations.

Visit Franklin Watts on the Internet at
http://publishing.grolier.com

Library of Congress Cataloging-in-Publication Data

Mania, Cathy.
    Woodpecker in the backyard / Cathy Mania and Robert C. Mania, Jr.
        p. cm. – (Wildlife conservation society books)
    Includes bibliographical references (p.).
    ISBN 0-531-11799-5    (lib. bdg.)            0-531-16527-2 (pbk.)
    1. Downy woodpecker--Juvenile literature. [1. Downy woodpecker. 2. Woodpecker.]
    I. Mania, Robert C. II. Title.

QL696.P56 M36        2000
598.7'2--dc21                                        00-042638

# Contents

# Meet the Authors

*Robert and Cathy Mania*

While they were researching and writing *Woodpecker in the Backyard*, **Robert** and **Cathy Mania** set up two cameras and tripods in their living room, on their balcony, and in their backyard. The Manias spent many hours observing and photographing woodpeckers, and kept careful notes of what they saw in a notebook. Since many of their observations were done outdoors during the winter, the Manias were pleased to learn that they could take pictures with their gloves on.

Robert Mania received bachelor's and master's degrees from Michigan Tech in Houghton, Michigan, and a Ph.D. in physics from Virginia Tech in Blacksburg, Virginia. He has taught at the college level for 19 years and is presently teaching physics and math at Kentucky State University in Frankfort, Kentucky. He has worked with middle school children who are advanced in their studies. He has also done research for the U.S. Army, Navy, and Air Force. Robert has written computer reviews for *PCM Magazine*, contributed to two science exam books, published eleven articles in technical journals, and prepared more than thirty U.S. Government Research Laboratory Reports.

*A page from the Manias' notebook*

# Robert and Cathy Mania's Home Town

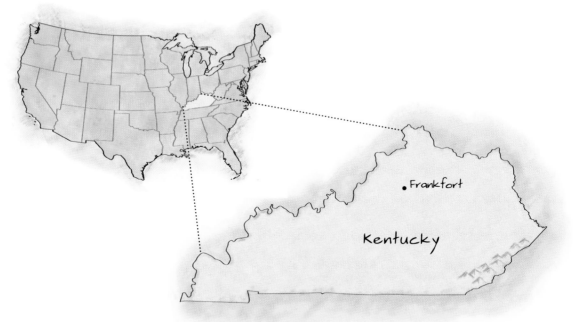

Frankfort

Kentucky

# Robert and Cathy Mania's Yard

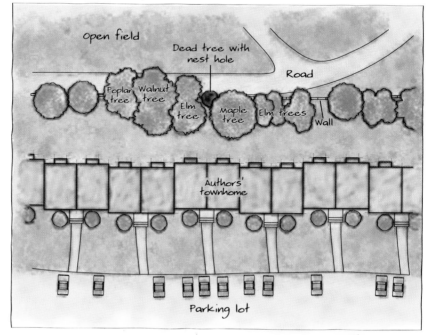

Open field

Dead tree with nest hole

Road

Poplar tree

Walnut tree

Elm tree

Maple tree

Elm trees

Wall

Authors' townhome

Parking lot

Cathy Mania received a bachelor's degree in math and a master's degree in higher education from Morehead State University in Morehead, Kentucky. In addition, she has recently received a bachelor's degree in studio arts from Kentucky State University, where she presently works as a laboratory assistant in the First-Year Experience Program.

Robert and Cathy's first children's book was *A Forest's Life*, which was published by Franklin Watts in 1997. They live in Frankfort, Kentucky, with their two children.

*Cathy Mania with her camera*

*A woodpecker taps on a tree in the authors' backyard.*

# Spotting a Downy

*On a sunny autumn morning, we hear a familiar tapping* sound in our backyard. A downy woodpecker is pecking softly at the trunk of a tree behind our house. As soon as we spot the little bird, it takes off. We stay perfectly still and listen intently. Soon we hear more tapping.

If we pay close attention, we can trace the wood-pecker's movements from tree to tree. It starts near the bottom of the poplar tree on the left side of the yard. As the downy jumps up the tree it moves in a zigzagging path. When it reaches the top of the poplar, it flies to the bottom of a nearby walnut tree. Then it moves on to an elm tree.

The woodpecker spends more time on the maple tree in our backyard. After moving up the trunk, the downy works its way along a branch and then rests in the sun with its back toward us. It turns its head to the side. Is it looking at us? The downy seems to be as curious about us as we are about it.

*The downy sits on top of a branch and warms up in the sun.*

This little bird is about 6 to 7 inches (15 to 17 centimeters) long from the tip of its bill to the end of its tail. It has a white head with black eye stripes, black check patches, and a black cap. The red spot on the back of its head tells us this downy is a male. Females do not have a red spot.

The downy has a tuft of fuzzy white feathers above its pointed black bill. This bunch of soft downlike feathers gives the woodpecker its name. The bird's chest and belly are white. Its tail is black, and its back is black with a broad white stripe down the center. The woodpecker's wings are black with rows of white spots.

# Downy Look-Alikes

It is easy to confuse a downy woodpecker with some of its close relatives. The yellow-bellied sapsucker looks similar. It is mostly black and white with red on the front of its head, and it is just a little larger than a downy. To tell these two birds apart, look for a long white stripe down the wings and pale yellow feathers just below the neck. If you see these markings, the bird is a yellow-bellied sapsucker.

The red-bellied woodpecker is even larger than the yellow-bellied sapsucker. It has rows of black and white stripes across its wings and back. The male has a red cap. Although it is called a red-bellied woodpecker, the red feathers on its belly are very faint and hard to see.

The pileated woodpecker is also black and white with red on its head, but it is much larger, about two or three times the size of a downy. It is easy to tell the pileated from the downy because the pileated has a red crest on its head and its back and wings have no white spots or stripes.

*The downy woodpecker eats insects that live inside trees.*

# Eat or Be Eaten

*Each time the male in our backyard flies to a new* tree, he lands a few feet above the ground and works in circles until he reaches the top. The hungry little bird is looking for his morning meal.

*Can you see this woodpecker's tongue?*

Tap, tap, tap. The woodpecker knocks on the trunk of a tree with his bill. Then he turns his head to the side and listens. Does the tree sound hollow inside? Maybe the bird hears insects tunneling underneath the bark.

The downy chips off the top layer of bark. When he sees beetles running for cover, he quickly laps them up. Downy woodpeckers have a long, sticky tongue with barbs on the end. This tongue is very useful for spearing insects and pulling them out of their tunnels. Sometimes a downy sticks its tongue into a hole even when it can't see its *prey*.

A woodpecker has a space inside its skull to store its long tongue. The tongue wraps around the brain just underneath the skull. When a woodpecker is hammering, its tongue acts as an extra layer of padding to protect its brain.

When the downy in our backyard has eaten all the insects within reach, he hops to a nearby branch. The acrobatic little bird hangs upside down and hammers his bill against the wood. How can woodpeckers bang into a tree and still hold on? The answer is simple—they have special feet and an unusual tail.

Many birds perch upright with their toes curled around a branch. They have three toes that point forward and one that points backward. A downy woodpecker's feet are different. It has two toes that point forward and two toes that point backward. The position of its toes helps the downy keep a firm grip on the tree.

A downy's tail has stiff feathers that end in spines. These spines dig into a tree when the wood-pecker leans back. Because its toes hang on while its tail presses against the tree, a downy does not lose its grip.

*A tree sparrow (left) perches with its toes curled around a branch. It has three toes pointing forward and one toe pointing backward. A downy woodpecker (right) clings to the side of a tree. It has two toes pointing forward and two toes pointing backward.*

Its special feet and tail help the downy woodpecker hunt for its main sources of food—adult insects, insect *larvae,* and insect eggs. A downy's favorite foods include ants, beetles, grubs, and caterpillars. (Grubs are the larvae of beetles. Caterpillars are the larvae of moths and butterflies.) Downies also eat seeds and fruit. They especially like raspberries, blackberries, and even the berries that grow on poison ivy plants.

*This downy has found a tasty treat.*

# Insect Control

You may think a woodpecker is damaging a tree when it drills into it or tears off the bark, but woodpeckers actually help trees stay

healthy. They are the only birds in North America that eat insects that live inside trees.

Woodpeckers search for dead and dying trees because they usually have insects inside. The insects are busy eating the rotting wood. When these insects move from one tree to another, they often carry diseases. By eating the insects, woodpeckers help prevent diseases from spreading through a forest.

Today, the woodpecker in our backyard spends most of his time hunting for beetles in the old trees behind our house. He is in continuous motion. He circles each tree by jumping sideways. Sometimes he jumps down the tree, but he can jump up the tree just as easily. He even appears to defy gravity by hopping along on the undersides of branches. Every once in a while, though, he stops pecking and searches for insects on leaves. The little downy has no trouble hopping around on the ends of tree branches.

As long as we are quiet, the downy continues to search for food. Even though adult woodpeckers have few enemies, the downy remains alert. We know that if we move too quickly or make too much noise, he will fly away.

Suddenly a red-shouldered hawk swoops into our yard and lands on the top branch of a tree. The woodpecker immediately stops his tapping. From its high perch, the hawk has a good view in all directions. It often sits in this tree for hours and watches for prey.

The hawk does not notice the smaller bird below. The way woodpeckers cling to trees makes them hard to see. For extra protection, the downy presses his neck against the tree. His colors blend with the tree bark, making him almost invisible. The woodpecker stays perfectly still for more than 30 minutes. Finally, the hawk leaves.

After the hawk is gone, the downy continues his search for food. He hops up one tree after another until he reaches the end of the line of trees in our backyard. Then he flies away across the large open

*The red-shouldered hawk is alert, watching for any movement below.*

field behind our house. With each flap of his wings, the downy is lifted upward. Between flaps, he dips downward. When he is flying, the downy looks like a boat bobbing up and down on the waves.

*The downy gets cold if it spends too much time outside of its roost hole in winter.*

# Through the Winter

*Like chickadees, nuthatches, and blue jays, downy* woodpeckers do not *migrate* to warm places in the winter. On cold nights, they sleep inside a dry *roost hole*. A downy woodpecker clings to the inside of its roost hole the same way it holds on to a tree trunk. Then it fluffs out its feathers, puts its bill under one wing, and falls asleep.

The downy in our backyard is a creature of habit. He goes into his roost hole at the same time every night and comes out at the same time every morning. As the winter grows colder, the downy spends more time in his warm, snug roost hole.

To get pictures of the downy, we have to adjust to the woodpecker's schedule. Every morning, we bundle up in our winter coats, hats, and gloves, set up our cameras on tripods, make adjustments for lighting and distance, and wait for him to show up.

When the woodpecker comes out, he searches for food and checks the borders of his *territory*. The downy stops at his favorite trees and hammers out

# Finding Woodpeckers

The best time to see woodpeckers is in the winter when the trees have no leaves. Woodpeckers cling close to tree trunks, so you have to look carefully to see the birds move. You may have better luck finding them if you listen for their tapping sound.

If you see trees with light-colored patches where the bark has been knocked off, a woodpecker has probably been there. Another way to spot a downy is too look for groups of noisy sparrows and black-capped chickadees. Downies often travel with these other birds in the winter.

a message that says, "Keep out!" When another downy flies into his territory, he quickly flies toward the intruder and chases it away.

During the winter, a downy woodpecker does not share its territory with other downies, but downies can live peacefully with other kinds of birds, including other kinds of woodpeckers. Because downies and red-bellied woodpeckers do not eat the same kind of insects, the downy in our backyard does not raise a fuss when a red-bellied woodpecker pays a visit.

The downy also gets along well with pileated woodpeckers. In fact, the downy sometimes follows a pileated woodpecker as it knocks

*The downy and a red-bellied woodpecker cling to the same tree.*

chunks of bark off trees. The smaller downy is not strong enough to knock off so much bark. The larger woodpecker's hard blows uncover insects deep inside the tree.

Winter is a lonely time for downies. The leaves have fallen from the trees and most of the insects are gone. Although food is scarce, the woodpeckers usually search for food in their own territories to avoid fights. A battle between two sharp-billed downies can cause serious injuries—or even death.

In the middle of February, we notice another woodpecker in our backyard. It is a female. We watch with excitement as one woodpecker follows the other up and down the trees. The

*This woodpecker does not have a red patch on the back of its head, so it is a female.*

birds are never close together, but they are often in the same tree.

When a second male comes into the yard, the first male flies toward it and bumps it. After a short burst of midair fighting, the second male flies away. Then the first male flies back to the tree where the female is hunting for insects. The two birds continue to search for food. When spring arrives, they will begin a new family.

*The male downy pauses. He is listening for his mate to answer his drum.*

# Drumming and Dancing

*Since male and female woodpeckers spend the* entire autumn and the beginning of the winter apart, you might wonder how they find one another in midwinter. They do it by *drumming*. Old hollow trees are usually the drums, and their bills are the drumsticks. When the neighborhood is quiet, this drumming can be heard over a long distance.

Woodpeckers drum by rapidly hammering their bills against hard objects, such as trees or poles. Dead branches or hollow trees make the loudest sounds. Sometimes woodpeckers drum on metal *gutters*. That makes a really loud sound!

Every male downy has a favorite drumming tree. He flies to that tree early in the morning and plays his own special rhythm. Then the bird pauses and listens for an answer from his mate. The downy looks to one side, and then to the other.  A moment later, he beats out his rhythm again.

The female hears the drumming call and leaves her roosting spot. She flies toward the male's territory, but

# A Woodpecker's Bill

The tip of a woodpecker's thick, strong bill is shaped like a chisel. It is perfect for chipping away at bark or drumming on a

hollow tree. Woodpeckers use their bills in other ways too. Some carry sunflower seeds—one at a time—to a crack in a tree or between rocks. Then they push the seed into the crack, and press the seed until it breaks open. Woodpeckers can also use their bill to make a nesting hole. Woodpeckers are usually peaceful birds, but sometimes they use their bills to fight.

Hammering into trees can wear out a woodpecker's bill, but that's no problem for these birds. As the end of the bill wears down, it is quickly replaced. Like your fingernails, a woodpecker's bill never stops growing.

*The female recognizes the rhythm of her mate's drumming.*

stops along the way to drum her own rhythm. This is her way of saying, "I'm awake! I hear you! I'm coming!"

Even after downies have mated, they will continue to drum. In the early morning, a downy woodpecker may drum out a greeting to a mate that has slept in a separate roost hole. If a downy dies, its mate may drum up to 100 times a day, trying to contact its missing partner or attract a new mate.

Downies also use vocal calls to find each other. Sometimes they call when they are disturbed or excited. They may scold softly at an intruder near their nest, or they may become very noisy if they feel threatened. The pair of downies in our backyard sometimes make busy, chirping sounds so soft that we cannot hear them unless they are very close to us.

Downies also use body movements to "talk" with one another. When another woodpecker is nearby, a downy may swing its head from side to side, move its head in a circle and thrust its bill forward, or raise the feathers on the top of its head. Sometimes a downy looks like it is dancing or fighting although it is not even touching the other bird.

When a downy turns its head to the side, another woodpecker can see the back of its head. Seeing a red patch there may help a female determine whether the other woodpecker is a healthy adult male.

Downies also identify one another by the white spots on their wings. That may be why downies sometimes bow, bob, and flutter their wings as they cling to a tree. Downies use body movements to send a message, just as people use speech.

*Look carefully at this downy's feathers. No two downies have the same pattern of spots.*

# Carpenters at Work

*After downy woodpeckers mate, they choose a place* for their nest. Most downies make a new *nest hole* every year. A new hole is cleaner and safer—at least until enemies find it.

Downies can make a nest hole in a tree, a post, or the wall of a house. They usually choose a dead or dying tree because rotting wood is softer and easier to dig into than healthy wood. Burned and diseased forests offer many good nesting sites for downies. The location of the nest hole is very important, so downies search for just the right place.

Many of the trees in our backyard are just right for a downy's nest hole. The birds fly from tree to tree to find the perfect spot. If one downy finds a good location, it drums to call its partner over. Sometimes one woodpecker begins to hammer out a hole and then the other comes to check it out.

The two eventually agree to make their nest hole in the trunk of a tree about 20 feet (6 m) above the ground. The male begins making the entrance to the

*This downy is making a new nest hole.*

nest underneath a large branch. The branch will act like a roof, protecting the nest from rain.

The male and female continue the work together, taking turns chipping away at the wood. As they work, tiny bits of wood fly in every direction. Each time one of the downies begins to hammer, it closes its eyes to keep out the sawdust and wood chips. The woodpecker's long, narrow nostrils are protected too. They are covered with feathers and hidden under a ridge on the bird's bill.

As the hole gets deeper, the downy digger backs out of the hole carrying some chips in its bill and tosses them to the ground. After working for about 20 minutes, it flies away and its mate arrives to continue the work.

Making a new nest hole may take up to a month, depending on how soft the wood is. When the woodpeckers finish, the entrance is a little more than 1 inch (2.5 cm) across—just big enough for one of them to squeeze through. If the downies made the entrance any larger, they might have to defend it against a larger bird.

When the woodpeckers in our backyard are done, their nest hole is more than 18 inches (46 cm) deep. It is wider inside, so there will be plenty of room for the chicks. This nest hole should keep the young downies safe from the neighbors' cats and other hungry *predators*.

*The downy begins digging a nest hole by drilling straight into the tree. Later he and his mate will dig downward to make a safe nest.*

# Where Downies Live

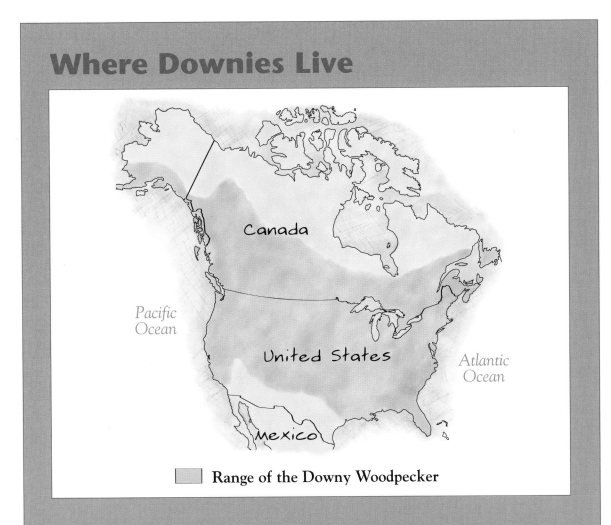

**Range of the Downy Woodpecker**

Although an individual downy does not travel far during its life-time, downies can be found throughout most of the United States and Canada. They live as far north as southern Alaska and as far south as Florida. Downies that live in the far north may migrate to warmer areas in the winter.

*The male waits until the female comes out of the nest hole. It is his turn to sit on the eggs.*

# Raising a Family

*The female downy sits quietly in the nest hole, keep-*ing her eggs warm and safe. She hears a slow, soft tapping on the tree outside. Her mate is back. There isn't enough room inside the nest hole for both adults, so the female woodpecker taps to let her mate know that she will come out.

As soon as the female emerges from the nest, the male downy goes in. The male and female woodpeckers take turns sitting on their small white eggs. We cannot see inside the nest hole, so we don't know how many eggs there are. Most female downies lay four or five eggs at a time.

After 12 days, the eggs hatch. The tiny chicks can't see yet, and they have no feathers. The nest hole is dark, quiet, and warm. It is a good place to sleep.

When the female comes into the nest hole, the hungry little *nestlings* cry out for food. She has brought them a worm. The female never flies very far from the nest, and she is always on the lookout for danger. The nestlings cannot protect themselves from hawks, weasels, snakes, or other enemies.

Some animals have no one to care for them, but the downies have two caring parents. During the day, the male spends his time traveling far from the nest hole to find food for the nestlings. Each time he leaves the nest, he carries out the babies' droppings.

*The male downy cleans out the nest hole.*

At night, the male sleeps with the chicks. His body keeps them warm, and his sharp bill is ready to fight off intruders.

The nestlings grow quickly. After a couple of weeks, they have feathers. They are beginning to look a lot like their parents. The young downies no longer wait at the bottom of the nest hole for their parents to bring food. Now they are strong enough to climb to the entrance and look around. There they can feel the breeze blowing and see the sun shining on the fluttering leaves. The nestlings aren't ready to venture outside the nest hole, though. They can't fly yet, and the ground is a long way down.

*This young downy will soon have the courage to fly out of the nest hole.*

# Increasing Numbers

The number of downies living in North America is increasing. Because a downy is smaller than other kinds of woodpeckers, it can find a suitable nesting site more easily. In addition, downies don't mind living near people. Downies are found wherever trees grow—in suburban neighborhoods, city parks, or anywhere else.

As the nestlings grow older, their parents bring them food less often. The young ones get hungry and restless. Finally, one of them flies out of the hole. Its first flight is strong and sure, and it lands safely on the branch of a nearby tree.

Soon our backyard is full of downy *fledglings*. It is unusual to see so many downies at one time. The fledglings look like their parents, only a little smaller. They follow their parents, fluttering their wings and calling. They are begging for food.

The parents feed the young ones and show them how to search for their own food. As parent and fledgling hammer together on a dead branch, the adult seems to be saying, "This is a good place, Junior. A lot of insects live in a dead branch like this one."

*The male still feeds the young downy even after it has left the nest.*

By the end of July, the fledglings have learned to feed themselves. Now, when the young meet one another—or their parents—they are no longer friendly. They raise the feathers on the tops of their heads and spread their wings and tails. It is time for each young downy to find its own territory and begin preparing for winter.

One of the young downies claims an old nest hole not far from the place where it was hatched. Another has flown farther away. Even though the young downy is only a few months old, it is busy making a roost hole for itself in an old tree.

Like their parents, the young downies will spend the long, cold winter sleeping, hunting for food, and patrolling their new territories. When spring arrives, they will drum out a rhythm to attract a mate. Then they will begin new woodpecker families of their own.

# Important Words

**drumming**  (verb) making a loud sound by beating against an object
(noun) the sound heard when a woodpecker beats its bill against a hollow tree or other object

**fledgling**  (noun) a young bird that has just left the nest

**gutter**  (noun) a groove or pipe along the roof of a house that catches rainwater

**larva**  (noun) the earliest life stage of an insect (plural larvae)

**migrate**  (verb) to travel a long distance at a particular time of year to find food or a mate

**nest hole**  (noun) the hole a woodpecker makes to lay eggs and raise its young

**nestling**  (noun) a chick that is too young to fly and spends most or all of its time in the nest

**predator**  (noun) an animal that hunts other animals for food

**prey**  (noun) an animal hunted by another animal for food

**roost hole**    (noun) a hole that a woodpecker sleeps in

**tapping**    (verb) making a soft, pecking sound, (noun or adjective) a soft, pecking sound made by a woodpecker

**territory**    (noun) an area that an animal defends against other animals

# To Find Out More

**Books**    Bailey, Jill and David Burnie. *Birds: DK Eyewitness Explorers*. New York: DK Publishing, Inc., 1997.

Green, Jen. *Learn About Birds*. New York: Lorenz Books, 1998.

Griggs, Jack. *All the Backyard Birds: East*. New York: HarperCollins, 1998.

_____. *All the Backyard Birds: West*. New York: HarperCollins, 1998.

Harrison, George. *Backyard Bird Watching for Kids*. Minocqua, Wisconsin: Willow Creek Press, 1997.

Stokes, Donald and Lillian Stokes. *Stokes Beginner's Guide to Birds: Western Region*. New York: Little, Brown and Company, 1996.

_____. *Stokes Beginner's Guide to Birds: Eastern Region*. New York: Little, Brown and Company, 1996.

## Organizations and Online Sites

**Canadian Wildlife Service**

*http://www.ec.gc.ca/cws-scf/hww-fap/dwpecker/dwpecker.html*

This site has information about Canadian wildlife, including the downy and other woodpeckers.

**HawkWatch International**

P.O. Box 660

Salt Lake City, UT 84110-0660

*http://www.hawkwatch.org/research_sites.html*

This site provides information about different kinds of hawks and other birds of prey.

**National Park Service**

United States Department of the Interior

Washington, DC 20013-7127

This site provides information about American parks and how to observe wildlife.

**National Audubon Society**

*http://www.audubon.org*

This site provides general information about bird-watching and bird conservation, including raptors, and provides links to other sites.

**U.S. Fish and Wildlife Service**

United States Department of the Interior

Washington, DC 20240

This site includes information on current environmental and conservation issues and their effects on animals.

**U.S. Forest Service**

United States Department of Agriculture

Washington, DC 20013

This site provides information about bird-watching as well as observing other kinds of animals and plants. It also provides links to other nature and education sites.

**Wildlife Conservation Society**

2300 Southern Blvd.

Bronx, NY 10460-1099

*http://www.wcs.org*

This site provides current information about environmental issues around the world.

# Index

**Photographs**© : Daybreak Imagery/Richard Day: 34, 36, 39; Dembinsky Photo Assoc.: cover (Sharon Cummings), 11 bottom (Dan Dempster), 17, 24 (Randall B. Henne); ENP Images/Steve Gettle: 12, 15 left, 30; Photo Researchers: 42 (John W. Bova), borders, back cover, 1 (S. W. Carter), 21, 37 (Doug Martin), 40 (S. Maslowski), 41 (O. S. Pettingill Jr.); Photodisc, Inc.: 9, 27, 31; Robert & Cathy Mania: 5, 8, 10; Tom Vezo: 11 top, 11 center, 15 right, 16, 19, 20; Visuals Unlimited: 38 (Mike Anich), 26 (John Gerlach), 13, 22, 29 (S. Maslowski), 23 (Tim Peterson), 28, 32 (Tom Ulrich).